THE SECOND BOOK
OF
ABC PUZZLES

THE SECOND BOOK
—— OF ——
ABC PUZZLES

KERMIT ROSE

authorHOUSE®

AuthorHouse™ LLC
1663 Liberty Drive
Bloomington, IN 47403
www.authorhouse.com
Phone: 1-800-839-8640

Published by AuthorHouse   09/24/2013

ISBN: 978-1-4918-2006-3 (sc)
ISBN: 978-1-4918-2007-0 (e)

Library of Congress Control Number: 2013917535

	1	2	3	4	5	6
1						
2						
3						
4						
5						
6						

In this six by six square diagram, each row and each column will contain exactly 2 A's, 2 B's, and 2 C's. This same rule will be true of the two diagonals of the diagram. Each cell of the 6 * 6 = 36 cells will contain exactly one letter. Thus after you find a few letters from the clues, you will be able to fill in the rest using the skills you developed solving the Sudoku puzzles

In the pages that follow, you will solve 90 puzzles that fill in this same diagram, using across and down clues. The row 1 clue applies only to row 1. The row 2 clue applies only to row 2. Etc.

These 90 puzzles come in 15 groups of six, with variable difficulty available in each group. This is achieved by each of the six puzzles in a group having the same answer, but different and complex ways of discovering it.

As such each group is labeled appropriately. For example, puzzle 16A, 16B, 16C, 16D, 16E, and 16F. Then the next group is 17A-17F, and so on. The puzzle numbers start with 16 because puzzle sets 1A through 15F are in my First Book of ABC Puzzles.

To elaborate what we mean by diagonals, the first diagonal refers to moving across the diagram by starting at the first square in the upper left hand corner and proceeding to the neighbor square below and to the right, which connects diagonally. Then continue downward diagonally until you reach the bottom, right square on the grid.
This is appropriately called a falling diagonal.

The second diagonal is obtained somewhat similarly, but this time you start from the *lower* left square on the grid, move to the square this one touches diagonally (at its *upper* right corner), and continue moving diagonally upwards till you reach the *top right* square.

This diagonal is then called a rising diagonal.

Visually, the two diagonals make a big "X" across the diagram.

In the pages that follow, you will solve 90 puzzles that fill in this same diagram, using across and down clues. The row 1 clue applies only to row 1. The row 2 clue applies only to row 2. Etc.

In the pages that follow, you will solve 90 puzzles that fill in this same diagram, using across and down clues. The row 1 clue applies only to row 1. The row 2 clue applies only to row 2. Etc.

These 90 puzzles come in 15 groups of six, with variable difficulty available in each group. This is achieved by each of the six puzzles in a group having the same answer, but different and complex ways of discovering it.

As such each group is labeled appropriately. For example, puzzle 16A, 16B, 16C, 16D, 16E, and 16F. Then the next group is 17A-17F, and so on. The puzzle numbers start with 16 because puzzle sets 1A through 15F are in my First Book of ABC Puzzles.

So, if you like easier puzzles then use the clues from all six puzzles, A, B, C, D, E and F at the same time. If you like puzzles of intermediate difficulty instead, try to solve one using the clues from only two or three of the puzzles within a group. It is a game of clues, and how much evidence you want to challenge yourself with is up to you.

Other fun puzzle books use different vocabularies to describe directions. So, let's get some jargon out of the way so that we are on the same page with what the clues mean. The given table provides this information as an easy reference, and its content becomes self-evident when using it to read through your first set of clues. It also includes reminders about what the difference is between a "rising" and "falling" diagonal on the diagram. In addition, notes about how the individual squares on the two different diagonals will be referenced to by number (square 1- square 6) are provided on the table.

Word Used in a Clue	What We Agree It Means
"before" in an across clue	"to the left of"
"after" in an across clue	"to the right of"
"first A" in an across clue	The A that is to the left of the second A
"first square" in an across clue	"left-most square"
"last square" in an across clue	"right-most square"
"before" in a down clue	"above"
"after" in a down clue	"below"
"first square" in a down clue	"top-most square"
"last square" in a down clue	"bottom-most square"
"falling diagonal"	refers to the diagonal going from upper left corner to lower right corner of the diagram
square number 1 of the falling diagonal	is the upper left corner square (the square you start from)
square number 6 of the falling diagonal	is the lower right corner square (the square you end on)
"rising diagonal"	refers to the diagonal going from lower left corner to upper right corner of the diagram
square number 1 of the rising diagonal	is the lower left corner square (the square you start from)
square number 6 of the rising diagonal	is the upper right corner square (the square you end on)

Note that "before" or "after" does not necessarily mean adjacent.

	1	2	3	4	5	6
1						
2						
3						
4						
5						
6						

ABC puzzle number 16A

How many clues will you require to solve the puzzle?

The better you are at solving this puzzle, the fewer clues you will need.

Row   Across

1   The number of letters between the A's is 0.

2   Second A is adjacent to first B.

3   First A comes after first B and second A comes after second B.

4   First B comes before second A.

5   The two A's are not adjacent.

6   Second C comes after first B.

Column   Down

1   Second A is not adjacent to second B.

2   Second C comes after second A.

3   First B is not adjacent to second C.

4   First C comes before second A.

5   First B comes before first A and second B comes before second A.

6   The first A is in square number 3.

Falling diagonal   The first square contains a B.

Rising diagonal   The second B is in square number 4.

	1	2	3	4	5	6
1						
2						
3						
4						
5						
6						

ABC puzzle number 16B

How many clues will you require to solve the puzzle?

The better you are at solving this puzzle, the fewer clues you will need.

Row   Across

1   Second A is not adjacent to second C.

2   The second C is in square number 5.

3   First A is not adjacent to first C.

4   Second A comes after first B.

5   Second C comes before second B.

6   The first square contains an A.

Column   Down

1   Second A comes after first B.

2   First C comes before second B.

3   The last square contains a B.

4   Second A comes after second C.

5   Second B is adjacent to second C.

6   First B comes before second A.

Falling diagonal   Second A comes before second B.

Rising diagonal   First A comes before first B and second A comes before second B.

	1	2	3	4	5	6
1						
2						
3						
4						
5						
6						

ABC puzzle number 16C

How many clues will you require to solve the puzzle?

The better you are at solving this puzzle, the fewer clues you will need.

Row   Across

1   Second C comes after second B.

2   First C comes after first A and second C comes after second A.

3   The first A is in square number 5.

4   The last square contains a B.

5   No two squares containing the same letter are adjacent.

6   First A is not adjacent to second B.

Column   Down

1   First B is not adjacent to second C.

2   The first A is adjacent to the second A and the first B is adjacent to the second B.

3   The first three consecutive squares will contain three different letters.

4   The two B's are not adjacent.

5   Second A is not adjacent to first C.

6   First C comes before second A.

Falling diagonal   Second B is not adjacent to first C.

Rising diagonal   First B comes before first C and second B comes before second C.

	1	2	3	4	5	6
1						
2						
3						
4						
5						
6						

ABC puzzle number 16D

How many clues will you require to solve the puzzle?

The better you are at solving this puzzle, the fewer clues you will need.

Row   Across

1   The second C is in square number 6.

2   First A is not adjacent to first C.

3   Second C comes before second B.

4   The first three consecutive squares will contain three different letters.

5   First A comes after second C.

6   The two B's are adjacent.

Column   Down

1   First A comes before First C.

2   First A is not adjacent to second B.

3   Second C comes after first A.

4   First A comes after first C and second A comes after second C.

5   First B comes before first C and second B comes after second C.

6   First A comes after first C.

Falling diagonal   Second A comes before second B.

Rising diagonal   The first B is in square number 2.

7

	1	2	3	4	5	6
1						
2						
3						
4						
5						
6						

ABC puzzle number 16E

How many clues will you require to solve the puzzle?

The better you are at solving this puzzle, the fewer clues you will need.

Row   Across

1   First position letter - second position letter + third position letter - fourth position letter + fifth position letter - sixth position letter = + (0A)+(2B)+(-2C).

2   The first B is in square number 3.

3   The two A's are adjacent.

4   First A comes after first C and second A comes before second C.

5   First A is not adjacent to first B.

6   Second C comes after second A.

Column   Down

1   First position letter - second position letter + third position letter - fourth position letter + fifth position letter - sixth position letter = + (-2A)+(2B)+(0C).

2   The number of letters between the C's is 2.

3   The number of letters between the C's is 1.

4   First B comes before first A and second B comes after second A.

5   The two C's are not adjacent.

6   Second A comes after first B.

Falling diagonal   First B comes before first C and second B comes before second C.

Rising diagonal   First A comes before second B.

	1	2	3	4	5	6
1						
2						
3						
4						
5						
6						

ABC puzzle number 16F

How many clues will you require to solve the puzzle?

The better you are at solving this puzzle, the fewer clues you will need.

Row	Across
1	Second A comes before second C.
2	The first B is in square number 3.
3	Second C comes before second B.
4	Second C comes after first B.
5	Second C comes before second A.
6	The two C's are not adjacent.

Column	Down
1	First A comes before first C and second A comes after second C.
2	First A is not adjacent to first B.
3	Second B is not adjacent to first C.
4	Neither the first square nor the last square will contain an A.
5	First A comes after first C and second A comes after second C.
6	The first A is in square number 3.

Falling diagonal	First A comes before second B.
Rising diagonal	First C comes after first A.

	1	2	3	4	5	6
1						
2						
3						
4						
5						
6						

ABC puzzle number 17A

How many clues will you require to solve the puzzle?

The better you are at solving this puzzle, the fewer clues you will need.

Row   Across

1   Second C comes after second A.

2   The second C is in square number 3.

3   First C comes before first B and second C comes before second B.

4   Neither the first square nor the last square will contain a B.

5   The first three consecutive squares will contain three different letters.

6   First B comes before first A.

Column   Down

1   Neither the first square nor the last square will contain an A.

2   First B comes before second C.

3   First C comes before second B.

4   First B is adjacent to first C.

5   First A comes after first B and second A comes after second B.

6   Second C comes after first B.

Falling diagonal   First A is adjacent to second B.

Rising diagonal   The number of letters between the C's is 4.

	1	2	3	4	5	6
1						
2						
3						
4						
5						
6						

ABC puzzle number 17B

How many clues will you require to solve the puzzle?

The better you are at solving this puzzle, the fewer clues you will need.

Row	Across
1	First B comes before second C.
2	First C comes before second A.
3	First C comes before first A.
4	First A comes before first C and second A comes after second C.
5	Neither the first square nor the last square will contain an A.
6	First C comes before first A and second C comes after second A.

Column	Down
1	The second A is in square number 4.
2	The second C is in square number 4.
3	Second A comes before first B.
4	First A comes after first B and second A comes after second B.
5	The second B is in square number 2.
6	Second A comes after first C.

Falling diagonal	Second C comes after second A.
Rising diagonal	First C comes before first B.

	1	2	3	4	5	6
1						
2						
3						
4						
5						
6						

ABC puzzle number 17C

How many clues will you require to solve the puzzle?

The better you are at solving this puzzle, the fewer clues you will need.

Row   Across

1   The two B's are not adjacent.

2   First C comes before second A.

3   The second C is in square number 5.

4   The two C's are not adjacent.

5   The first three consecutive squares will contain three different letters.

6   The number of letters between the C's is 4.

Column   Down

1   The second C is in square number 6.

2   First position letter - second position letter + third position letter - fourth position letter + fifth position letter - sixth position letter = + (2A)+(0B)+(-2C).

3   First C comes before second A.

4   First C comes before first B.

5   Second C comes before second A.

6   First C comes before second A.

Falling diagonal   Second B is not adjacent to first C.

Rising diagonal   The two B's are not adjacent.

	1	2	3	4	5	6
1						
2						
3						
4						
5						
6						

ABC puzzle number 17D

How many clues will you require to solve the puzzle?

The better you are at solving this puzzle, the fewer clues you will need.

Row   Across

1   First B comes before first A.

2   Second C comes before first B.

3   Second A comes after first B.

4   The first three consecutive squares will contain three different letters.

5   First A comes before first C and second A comes after second C.

6   The first and last squares will contain a C.

Column   Down

1   Second B is adjacent to second C.

2   Second C comes after first B.

3   Neither the first square nor the last square will contain a C.

4   First A is adjacent to second B.

5   First B comes before first A and second B comes before second A.

6   First B is not adjacent to second C.

Falling diagonal   Neither the first square nor the last square will contain an A.

Rising diagonal   First B comes before second C.

	1	2	3	4	5	6
1						
2						
3						
4						
5						
6						

ABC puzzle number 17E

How many clues will you require to solve the puzzle?

The better you are at solving this puzzle, the fewer clues you will need.

Row	Across
1	Second A comes before first C.
2	First A is not adjacent to second B.
3	The two C's are not adjacent.
4	Second A is not adjacent to second B.
5	Neither the first square nor the last square will contain an A.
6	First B comes after First C.

Column	Down
1	Second A is not adjacent to first B.
2	The second C is in square number 4.
3	Second B is not adjacent to first C.
4	First C comes before first B.
5	The first square contains a B.
6	Second C comes after second A.

Falling diagonal	First A comes before second B.
Rising diagonal	The first and last squares will contain a C.

	1	2	3	4	5	6
1						
2						
3						
4						
5						
6						

ABC puzzle number 17F

How many clues will you require to solve the puzzle?

The better you are at solving this puzzle, the fewer clues you will need.

Row   Across

1   The number of letters between the A's is 0.

2   First B comes after first A.

3   First A is not adjacent to second C.

4   Second A comes after second C.

5   First A comes before First C.

6   First C comes before second A.

Column   Down

1   The number of letters between the B's is 3.

2   First position letter - second position letter + third position letter - fourth position letter + fifth position letter - sixth position letter = + (2A)+(0B)+(-2C).

3   First B comes after first C and second B comes after second C.

4   Neither the first square nor the last square will contain a B.

5   First B is not adjacent to second C.

6   First B comes after first A.

Falling diagonal   Neither the first square nor the last square will contain an A.

Rising diagonal   The second B is in square number 5.

	1	2	3	4	5	6
1						
2						
3						
4						
5						
6						

ABC puzzle number 18A

How many clues will you require to solve the puzzle?

The better you are at solving this puzzle, the fewer clues you will need.

Row	Across
1	Second A comes before first B.
2	First C comes before first B.
3	First B is not adjacent to second C.
4	The first A is in square number 5.
5	First A is adjacent to second C.
6	The first three consecutive squares will contain three different letters.

Column	Down
1	First C comes before second B.
2	Neither the first square nor the last square will contain a C.
3	First B comes before first A and second B comes before second A.
4	The second A is in square number 6.
5	First B comes after first A and second B comes after second A.
6	Second C comes before second A.

Falling diagonal   First C comes before first B and second C comes before second B.

Rising diagonal   First position letter - second position letter + third position letter - fourth position letter + fifth position letter - sixth position letter = + (0A)+(2B)+(-2C).

	1	2	3	4	5	6
1						
2						
3						
4						
5						
6						

ABC puzzle number 18B

How many clues will you require to solve the puzzle?

The better you are at solving this puzzle, the fewer clues you will need.

Row   Across

1   First B comes before first C.

2   Second B is not adjacent to second C.

3   First A comes after first C and second A comes before second C.

4   The second A is in square number 6.

5   Second C comes before second A.

6   The first C is in square number 3.

Column   Down

1   First C comes before first B and second C comes before second B.

2   First B comes before second C.

3   Second A comes after first C.

4   The first A is in square number 3.

5   The second B is in square number 5.

6   Second A is not adjacent to second C.

Falling diagonal   The second B is in square number 6.

Rising diagonal   First A comes after first B.

	1	2	3	4	5	6
1						
2						
3						
4						
5						
6						

ABC puzzle number 18C

How many clues will you require to solve the puzzle?

The better you are at solving this puzzle, the fewer clues you will need.

Row   Across

1   First C comes after first B and second C comes after second B.

2   First B comes after First C.

3   Second A comes before second B.

4   Second A is not adjacent to first B.

5   First C comes before first A.

6   First B comes before first A.

Column   Down

1   The first A is in square number 1.

2   The number of letters between the B's is 0.

3   First A is adjacent to first C.

4   First A is not adjacent to second C.

5   The second B is in square number 5.

6   The number of letters between the C's is 1.

Falling diagonal   First A is not adjacent to second B.

Rising diagonal   Second C comes after first A.

	1	2	3	4	5	6
1						
2						
3						
4						
5						
6						

ABC puzzle number 18D

How many clues will you require to solve the puzzle?

The better you are at solving this puzzle, the fewer clues you will need.

Row   Across

1   The number of letters between the A's is 0.

2   Second A is not adjacent to second C.

3   First A comes before second B.

4   Second A comes after first B.

5   The number of letters between the C's is 1.

6   Second A comes after first C.

Column   Down

1   First A is not adjacent to second B.

2   First A comes before first C and second A comes after second C.

3   The first C is in square number 2.

4   The first C is in square number 4.

5   First B comes after first A.

6   Second B is not adjacent to first C.

Falling diagonal   The two B's are adjacent.

Rising diagonal   First B is adjacent to first C.

19

	1	2	3	4	5	6
1						
2						
3						
4						
5						
6						

ABC puzzle number 18E

How many clues will you require to solve the puzzle?

The better you are at solving this puzzle, the fewer clues you will need.

Row   Across

1   First A is not adjacent to second B.

2   First A comes before first B.

3   First B comes before second C.

4   First A comes after first B and second A comes after second B.

5   The first three consecutive squares will contain three different letters.

6   Second C comes before second B.

Column   Down

1   Second C comes before first B.

2   First A comes before second B.

3   The first B is in square number 1.

4   Neither the first square nor the last square will contain a C.

5   Second A comes after first C.

6   Second A is not adjacent to first C.

Falling diagonal   First B comes after second C.

Rising diagonal   Second A is not adjacent to first B.

	1	2	3	4	5	6
1						
2						
3						
4						
5						
6						

ABC puzzle number 18F

How many clues will you require to solve the puzzle?

The better you are at solving this puzzle, the fewer clues you will need.

Row   Across

1   First C comes after first B and second C comes after second B.

2   First A is not adjacent to second B.

3   First A comes after first C.

4   Second C comes after first B.

5   The second C is in square number 4.

6   Second C comes after first A.

Column   Down

1   First B is adjacent to second C.

2   First A comes before first C and second A comes after second C.

3   Second A is not adjacent to first C.

4   The last square contains an A.

5   Second C comes after first A.

6   First A comes after first C and second A comes after second C.

Falling diagonal   Second A is adjacent to second C.

Rising diagonal   Second A is not adjacent to first B.

	1	2	3	4	5	6
1						
2						
3						
4						
5						
6						

ABC puzzle number 19A

How many clues will you require to solve the puzzle?

The better you are at solving this puzzle, the fewer clues you will need.

Row   Across

1   Second B is not adjacent to second C.

2   The two B's are not adjacent.

3   Second A is not adjacent to first B.

4   First A comes after first C and second A comes after second C.

5   First B is adjacent to first C.

6   First A is not adjacent to first C.

Column   Down

1   First B comes before second A.

2   Second B is adjacent to second C.

3   First C comes after first B and second C comes before second B.

4   The first three consecutive squares will contain three different letters.

5   The first three consecutive squares will contain three different letters.

6   First C comes before first B.

Falling diagonal   Second B is adjacent to second C.

Rising diagonal   First A is not adjacent to first C.

	1	2	3	4	5	6
1						
2						
3						
4						
5						
6						

ABC puzzle number 19B

How many clues will you require to solve the puzzle?

The better you are at solving this puzzle, the fewer clues you will need.

Row   Across

1   The two B's are adjacent.

2   First B comes after First C.

3   The first three consecutive squares will contain three different letters.

4   The first C is in square number 2.

5   Second B is adjacent to second C.

6   The first B is in square number 3.

Column   Down

1   First B is not adjacent to second C.

2   First A comes after first B.

3   First C comes after first A.

4   Second B is adjacent to second C.

5   First A comes before second B.

6   Second B is not adjacent to first C.

Falling diagonal   Neither the first square nor the last square will contain a B.

Rising diagonal   Second A comes after first B.

	1	2	3	4	5	6
1						
2						
3						
4						
5						
6						

ABC puzzle number 19C

How many clues will you require to solve the puzzle?

The better you are at solving this puzzle, the fewer clues you will need.

Row   Across

1   Second B is not adjacent to first C.

2   First C comes before second B.

3   The first and last squares will contain a B.

4   The second C is in square number 3.

5   First A comes after first C.

6   First A comes before first B and second A comes before second B.

Column   Down

1   First C comes before second A.

2   The number of letters between the B's is 2.

3   First C comes before second B.

4   First C comes before first A and second C comes after second A.

5   The two B's are not adjacent.

6   The first and last squares will contain a C.

Falling diagonal   First A comes before first C and second A comes before second C.

Rising diagonal   First A is not adjacent to first C.

	1	2	3	4	5	6
1						
2						
3						
4						
5						
6						

ABC puzzle number 19D

How many clues will you require to solve the puzzle?

The better you are at solving this puzzle, the fewer clues you will need.

Row	Across
1	First A comes before first B and second A comes after second B.
2	First A comes after first C.
3	The number of letters between the A's is 1.
4	The two B's are not adjacent.
5	First B comes before first A and second B comes before second A.
6	First B is not adjacent to first C.

Column	Down
1	First position letter - second position letter + third position letter - fourth position letter + fifth position letter - sixth position letter = + (0A)+(0B)+(0C).
2	First A comes after first B.
3	Second A is adjacent to second C.
4	First C comes after first B.
5	The first B is in square number 2.
6	The two C's are not adjacent.

| Falling diagonal | Neither the first square nor the last square will contain a B. |
| Rising diagonal | Second A is not adjacent to second C. |

	1	2	3	4	5	6
1						
2						
3						
4						
5						
6						

ABC puzzle number 19E

How many clues will you require to solve the puzzle?

The better you are at solving this puzzle, the fewer clues you will need.

Row   Across

1   First B comes after first C and second B comes before second C.

2   First B is not adjacent to second C.

3   First B comes before second C.

4   First position letter - second position letter + third position letter - fourth position letter + fifth position letter - sixth position letter = + (0A)+(0B)+(0C).

5   First C comes before first B and second C comes before second B.

6   Second B is not adjacent to second C.

Column   Down

1   First A comes before first C and second A comes after second C.

2   First A is not adjacent to second B.

3   Second C comes before second A.

4   The number of letters between the A's is 0.

5   First A comes before second C.

6   The two C's are not adjacent.

Falling diagonal   The second C is in square number 6.

Rising diagonal   Second A comes before second C.

	1	2	3	4	5	6
1						
2						
3						
4						
5						
6						

ABC puzzle number 19F

How many clues will you require to solve the puzzle?

The better you are at solving this puzzle, the fewer clues you will need.

Row   Across

1   First A comes before first B and second A comes after second B.

2   First A is not adjacent to first C.

3   First B comes before first C and second B comes after second C.

4   First B comes before first A.

5   First A comes after first C.

6   Every group of three consecutive squares will contain two of the same letter.

Column   Down

1   The second C is in square number 5.

2   Second A comes after first B.

3   The first A is in square number 2.

4   Neither the first square nor the last square will contain a C.

5   The two C's are not adjacent.

6   Neither the first square nor the last square will contain an A.

Falling diagonal   First A comes before First C.

Rising diagonal   Second C comes after first B.

27

	1	2	3	4	5	6
1						
2						
3						
4						
5						
6						

ABC puzzle number 20A

How many clues will you require to solve the puzzle?

The better you are at solving this puzzle, the fewer clues you will need.

Row   Across

1   Second A comes after first C.

2   First B comes before first A and second B comes before second A.

3   First B comes after First C.

4   First B comes after first A.

5   First C comes before second B.

6   Second C comes after second B.

Column   Down

1   Neither the first square nor the last square will contain a C.

2   Second C comes after second B.

3   First A comes after first B and second A comes after second B.

4   First B comes after First C.

5   Second B is not adjacent to first C.

6   The first A is in square number 1.

Falling diagonal   First C comes before second B.

Rising diagonal   First B comes before first A.

	1	2	3	4	5	6
1						
2						
3						
4						
5						
6						

ABC puzzle number 20B

How many clues will you require to solve the puzzle?

The better you are at solving this puzzle, the fewer clues you will need.

Row   Across

1   The number of letters between the C's is 0.

2   Second C comes after second B.

3   Second A comes before first B.

4   First A comes after first C.

5   Second A is not adjacent to first B.

6   The number of letters between the A's is 0.

Column   Down

1   First B comes after second C.

2   Neither the first square nor the last square will contain an A.

3   The second C is in square number 5.

4   Second A comes after first C.

5   The number of letters between the C's is 2.

6   First B is not adjacent to second C.

Falling diagonal   First B comes before second C.

Rising diagonal   First B is adjacent to first C.

	1	2	3	4	5	6
1						
2						
3						
4						
5						
6						

ABC puzzle number 20C

How many clues will you require to solve the puzzle?

The better you are at solving this puzzle, the fewer clues you will need.

Row   Across

1   Second A comes after second B.

2   The first B is in square number 2.

3   The first square contains an A.

4   Second A comes after first C.

5   First C comes before first A and second C comes before second A.

6   First B is adjacent to first C.

Column   Down

1   First A is not adjacent to second B.

2   The second B is in square number 2.

3   First B comes before second C.

4   First C comes before first B.

5   First C comes before first A.

6   Second C comes after first B.

Falling diagonal   First A is not adjacent to second C.

Rising diagonal   Some group of three consecutive squares will contain three of the
                        same letter.

	1	2	3	4	5	6
1						
2						
3						
4						
5						
6						

ABC puzzle number 20D

How many clues will you require to solve the puzzle?

The better you are at solving this puzzle, the fewer clues you will need.

Row   Across

1   First B is not adjacent to second C.

2   The number of letters between the B's is 1.

3   The two A's are adjacent.

4   Second A comes after second B.

5   The second C is in square number 3.

6   Second C comes after first A.

Column   Down

1   First C comes before first B.

2   First A comes before First C.

3   First B comes before second C.

4   First B comes after First C.

5   The first C is in square number 1.

6   Second A comes before second C.

Falling diagonal   First A comes before First C.

Rising diagonal   The number of letters between the B's is 1.

	1	2	3	4	5	6
1						
2						
3						
4						
5						
6						

ABC puzzle number 20E

How many clues will you require to solve the puzzle?

The better you are at solving this puzzle, the fewer clues you will need.

Row   Across

1   First A is not adjacent to second C.

2   The first C is in square number 1.

3   Second B is not adjacent to second C.

4   First A is adjacent to first B.

5   First C comes before second B.

6   The two A's are adjacent.

Column   Down

1   First B comes after second A.

2   The two C's are adjacent.

3   Second B is adjacent to second C.

4   The first A is in square number 5.

5   First position letter - second position letter + third position letter - fourth position letter + fifth position letter - sixth position letter = + (0A)+(0B)+(0C).

6   The first A is in square number 1.

Falling diagonal   First C comes before second B.

Rising diagonal   First B comes before first A.

	1	2	3	4	5	6
1						
2						
3						
4						
5						
6						

ABC puzzle number 20F

How many clues will you require to solve the puzzle?

The better you are at solving this puzzle, the fewer clues you will need.

Row   Across

1   First C comes before second A.

2   First position letter - second position letter + third position letter - fourth position letter + fifth position letter - sixth position letter = + (2A)+(-2B)+(0C).

3   First A comes before second B.

4   First A comes before first B and second A comes after second B.

5   First A comes after first B.

6   The first A is adjacent to the second A.

Column   Down

1   First C comes after first A.

2   First C comes after second B.

3   First B is not adjacent to first C.

4   The number of letters between the C's is 1.

5   First A comes before first B and second A comes before second B.

6   The last square contains a C.

Falling diagonal   Second A is not adjacent to first B.

Rising diagonal   Second C comes before first A.

	1	2	3	4	5	6
1						
2						
3						
4						
5						
6						

ABC puzzle number 21A

How many clues will you require to solve the puzzle?

The better you are at solving this puzzle, the fewer clues you will need.

Row   Across

1   First B comes before second C.

2   Neither the first square nor the last square will contain an A.

3   First A comes before first B and second A comes after second B.

4   The number of letters between the B's is 2.

5   The number of letters between the A's is 0.

6   Second C comes before second A.

Column   Down

1   Second A comes after second C.

2   First B comes before second C.

3   Second C comes after second B.

4   First B comes after First C.

5   Second A is not adjacent to second C.

6   First C comes before first B.

Falling diagonal   First B comes before first C.

Rising diagonal   First C comes after first A and second C comes before second A.

	1	2	3	4	5	6
1						
2						
3						
4						
5						
6						

ABC puzzle number 21B

How many clues will you require to solve the puzzle?

The better you are at solving this puzzle, the fewer clues you will need.

Row   Across

1   First A is not adjacent to first B.

2   The number of letters between the B's is 1.

3   Second C comes after second B.

4   First A comes before first B and second A comes before second B.

5   First C comes before first A.

6   Second A comes after first B.

Column   Down

1   Second C comes after first B.

2   The second C is in square number 6.

3   The two B's are not adjacent.

4   First B comes after First C.

5   Second A is not adjacent to second B.

6   First B is adjacent to second C.

Falling diagonal   The second C is in square number 4.

Rising diagonal   The first B is adjacent to the second B.

	1	2	3	4	5	6
1						
2						
3						
4						
5						
6						

ABC puzzle number 21C

How many clues will you require to solve the puzzle?

The better you are at solving this puzzle, the fewer clues you will need.

Row	Across
1	First A is not adjacent to second C.
2	Some group of three consecutive squares will contain three of the same letter.
3	First B is not adjacent to second C.
4	The last square contains a B.
5	The two B's are adjacent.
6	The first B is adjacent to the second B and the first C is adjacent to the second C.

Column	Down
1	Neither the first square nor the last square will contain a C.
2	First A comes before first C and second A comes before second C.
3	The first A is in square number 1.
4	First B comes after first A and second B comes after second A.
5	Second C comes before first A.
6	The first C is in square number 2.

Falling diagonal	First B comes before first C.
Rising diagonal	Second A is not adjacent to first C.

	1	2	3	4	5	6
1						
2						
3						
4						
5						
6						

ABC puzzle number 21D

How many clues will you require to solve the puzzle?

The better you are at solving this puzzle, the fewer clues you will need.

Row	Across
1	Second A is not adjacent to first B.
2	First A is not adjacent to first C.
3	Second A is not adjacent to first B.
4	Second A comes after first C.
5	The first square contains a C.
6	First A is not adjacent to first B.

Column	Down
1	First A comes after first B and second A comes after second B.
2	The number of letters between the B's is 1.
3	Second A is not adjacent to first C.
4	First C comes before second A.
5	First position letter - second position letter + third position letter - fourth position letter + fifth position letter - sixth position letter = + (0A)+(0B)+(0C).
6	The two C's are adjacent.

Falling diagonal	Second C comes before second A.
Rising diagonal	First C comes before first B.

	1	2	3	4	5	6
1						
2						
3						
4						
5						
6						

ABC puzzle number 21E

How many clues will you require to solve the puzzle?

The better you are at solving this puzzle, the fewer clues you will need.

Row   Across

1   Some group of three consecutive squares will contain three of the same letter.

2   Second A is not adjacent to first B.

3   Second A is not adjacent to first B.

4   Second A comes after second C.

5   First A is not adjacent to first C.

6   The number of letters between the A's is 4.

Column   Down

1   First C comes after first A.

2   Second C comes after first A.

3   The number of letters between the A's is 3.

4   First B comes after first A.

5   First B comes after first C and second B comes after second C.

6   First A is not adjacent to second B.

Falling diagonal   The first C is in square number 3.

Rising diagonal   Second B is not adjacent to first C.

	1	2	3	4	5	6
1						
2						
3						
4						
5						
6						

ABC puzzle number 21F

How many clues will you require to solve the puzzle?

The better you are at solving this puzzle, the fewer clues you will need.

Row   Across

1   First B is not adjacent to first C.

2   The two C's are adjacent.

3   First B comes before first C and second B comes before second C.

4   First C comes before second B.

5   First A comes after first C.

6   First A comes before first C and second A comes after second C.

Column   Down

1   Second C comes after second B.

2   The second A is in square number 4.

3   Second A is adjacent to second C.

4   Second C comes before second A.

5   The number of letters between the C's is 0.

6   The second C is in square number 3.

Falling diagonal   Second A comes after first C.

Rising diagonal   First A comes before second C.

	1	2	3	4	5	6
1						
2						
3						
4						
5						
6						

ABC puzzle number 22A

How many clues will you require to solve the puzzle?

The better you are at solving this puzzle, the fewer clues you will need.

Row   Across

1   First C comes after first A.

2   First B is not adjacent to second C.

3   First A comes before first C and second A comes before second C.

4   There exist three consecutive squares which contain three different letters.

5   First A comes after first B and second A comes before second B.

6   First B comes after first C and second B comes after second C.

Column   Down

1   First A comes after first B and second A comes before second B.

2   Second A comes after first C.

3   The first C is in square number 3.

4   The two A's are not adjacent.

5   First A comes after first B.

6   Second A is not adjacent to first C.

Falling diagonal   First A comes after first B.

Rising diagonal   The two C's are not adjacent.

	1	2	3	4	5	6
1						
2						
3						
4						
5						
6						

ABC puzzle number 22B

How many clues will you require to solve the puzzle?

The better you are at solving this puzzle, the fewer clues you will need.

Clues

Row   Across

1   Second C comes after second B.

2   First A comes before second B.

3   The two A's are not adjacent.

4   First B is not adjacent to first C.

5   First B is not adjacent to second C.

6   First C comes before first A.

Column   Down

1   The two B's are not adjacent.

2   First C comes after first B.

3   The second C is in square number 4.

4   The second C is in square number 5.

5   The first three consecutive squares will contain three different letters.

6   Second A comes after second C.

Falling diagonal   First A comes before second C.

Rising diagonal   First A is not adjacent to second B.

	1	2	3	4	5	6
1						
2						
3						
4						
5						
6						

ABC puzzle number 22C

How many clues will you require to solve the puzzle?

The better you are at solving this puzzle, the fewer clues you will need.

Row   Across

1   First A comes before second B.

2   First A is not adjacent to second B.

3   First A comes before first B.

4   First A comes before second B.

5   Neither the first square nor the last square will contain an A.

6   The second B is in square number 4.

Column   Down

1   The two B's are not adjacent.

2   The last square contains a C.

3   The first B is in square number 1.

4   First B comes before second A.

5   The second C is in square number 5.

6   First A comes before First C.

Falling diagonal   Some group of three consecutive squares will contain three of the
                          same letter.

Rising diagonal   The two A's are not adjacent.

	1	2	3	4	5	6
1						
2						
3						
4						
5						
6						

ABC puzzle number 22D

How many clues will you require to solve the puzzle?

The better you are at solving this puzzle, the fewer clues you will need.

Row   Across

1   First B comes before first A.

2   First A is not adjacent to second C.

3   First C comes after first B.

4   Second A comes after first C.

5   Second B is not adjacent to first C.

6   Neither the first square nor the last square will contain a B.

Column   Down

1   First B comes before first C.

2   Second C comes after second A.

3   First A comes after first B.

4   The last square contains a B.

5   Second B is adjacent to second C.

6   Second A is not adjacent to first B.

Falling diagonal   The two A's are not adjacent.

Rising diagonal   The last square contains an A.

	1	2	3	4	5	6
1						
2						
3						
4						
5						
6						

ABC puzzle number 22E

How many clues will you require to solve the puzzle?

The better you are at solving this puzzle, the fewer clues you will need.

Row   Across

1   Second C comes before second A.

2   First position letter - second position letter + third position letter - fourth position letter + fifth position letter - sixth position letter = + (0A)+(0B)+(0C).

3   Second C comes after second B.

4   First C comes after first A and second C comes before second A.

5   First A comes before second B.

6   First A comes after first C and second A comes after second C.

Column   Down

1   Second A comes before second B.

2   First C comes after first B and second C comes after second B.

3   The two B's are not adjacent.

4   First B comes before second C.

5   The second A is in square number 6.

6   Second B is not adjacent to first C.

Falling diagonal   First A comes after second B.

Rising diagonal   Second C comes before first B.

	1	2	3	4	5	6
1						
2						
3						
4						
5						
6						

ABC puzzle number 22F

How many clues will you require to solve the puzzle?

The better you are at solving this puzzle, the fewer clues you will need.

Row   Across

1   First position letter - second position letter + third position letter - fourth position letter + fifth position letter - sixth position letter = + (-2A)+(2B)+(0C).

2   Second A comes after first B.

3   First A is not adjacent to second C.

4   Second A is not adjacent to second B.

5   The number of letters between the A's is 0.

6   The first C is in square number 1.

Column   Down

1   Second B is not adjacent to first C.

2   First B comes before second C.

3   Second A is adjacent to second B.

4   The last square contains a B.

5   The first A is in square number 3.

6   Second B is not adjacent to first C.

Falling diagonal   First C comes after first B and second C comes after second B.

Rising diagonal   The second A is in square number 6.

	1	2	3	4	5	6
1						
2						
3						
4						
5						
6						

ABC puzzle number 23A

How many clues will you require to solve the puzzle?

The better you are at solving this puzzle, the fewer clues you will need.

Row   Across

1   First B comes after first C and second B comes after second C.

2   First C comes after first B.

3   First C comes before second B.

4   First A comes before second B.

5   First B is not adjacent to second C.

6   First B comes before first A and second B comes after second A.

Column   Down

1   Second C comes after second A.

2   The number of letters between the A's is 2.

3   Second C comes after first A.

4   Second B is adjacent to first C.

5   First A comes before second C.

6   The second B is in square number 5.

Falling diagonal   The second A is in square number 5.

Rising diagonal   First B comes before second C.

	1	2	3	4	5	6
1						
2						
3						
4						
5						
6						

ABC puzzle number 23B

How many clues will you require to solve the puzzle?

The better you are at solving this puzzle, the fewer clues you will need.

Row	Across
1	First A comes after first B and second A comes before second B.
2	First B comes before second C.
3	The first three consecutive squares will contain three different letters.
4	First A comes before second B.
5	First B is not adjacent to first C.
6	The first C is in square number 1.

Column	Down
1	The number of letters between the B's is 2.
2	The second B is in square number 6.
3	First C comes before second B.
4	Second B is adjacent to first C.
5	Second A comes before second B.
6	The first A is in square number 3.

Falling diagonal   The first C is in square number 1.

Rising diagonal   First A is not adjacent to second B.

47

	1	2	3	4	5	6
1						
2						
3						
4						
5						
6						

ABC puzzle number 23C

How many clues will you require to solve the puzzle?

The better you are at solving this puzzle, the fewer clues you will need.

Row   Across

1   Second A is not adjacent to second B.

2   Second A comes after second B.

3   First B is adjacent to second C.

4   The first A is in square number 1.

5   Second A is adjacent to second B.

6   First A comes after first B and second A comes before second B.

Column   Down

1   First B comes before first A and second B comes after second A.

2   The first C is in square number 3.

3   The first B is in square number 3.

4   First A comes before second B.

5   First C comes before second A.

6   First B comes before first A and second B comes after second A.

Falling diagonal   First A comes after first C.

Rising diagonal   First C comes before first A.

	1	2	3	4	5	6
1						
2						
3						
4						
5						
6						

ABC puzzle number 23D

How many clues will you require to solve the puzzle?

The better you are at solving this puzzle, the fewer clues you will need.

Row   Across

1   First C comes before first A.

2   First B comes before second C.

3   First C comes after first A.

4   Second A comes after first B.

5   The first B is in square number 1.

6   Second C comes after first A.

Column   Down

1   Second B is not adjacent to first C.

2   The two B's are not adjacent.

3   Second A is not adjacent to second B.

4   Second A is not adjacent to second B.

5   First C comes before first A and second C comes before second A.

6   Second C comes after second B.

Falling diagonal   First A is not adjacent to second C.

Rising diagonal   First A is not adjacent to second B.

	1	2	3	4	5	6
1						
2						
3						
4						
5						
6						

ABC puzzle number 23E

How many clues will you require to solve the puzzle?

The better you are at solving this puzzle, the fewer clues you will need.

Row   Across

1   First C comes before second A.

2   First A comes before second B.

3   Second C comes after first B.

4   First C comes before first B.

5   First A comes before second C.

6   The number of letters between the C's is 4.

Column   Down

1   The second A is in square number 4.

2   First B is not adjacent to first C.

3   First A comes before First C.

4   First A is adjacent to first B.

5   First C comes before second B.

6   First A comes before second C.

Falling diagonal   Second A comes after first C.

Rising diagonal   First position letter - second position letter + third position letter - fourth position letter + fifth position letter - sixth position letter = +(0A)+(0B)+(0C).

	1	2	3	4	5	6
1						
2						
3						
4						
5						
6						

ABC puzzle number 23F

How many clues will you require to solve the puzzle?

The better you are at solving this puzzle, the fewer clues you will need.

Row   Across

1   The second B is in square number 6.

2   Neither the first square nor the last square will contain an A.

3   Second C comes after first B.

4   The two B's are adjacent.

5   First B comes before first A.

6   The first and last squares will contain a C.

Column   Down

1   First A comes after first C.

2   Second A is not adjacent to first C.

3   First C comes after first A.

4   The two C's are not adjacent.

5   The two B's are not adjacent.

6   Second A comes after first C.

Falling diagonal   The two B's are adjacent.

Rising diagonal   First C comes before second A.

	1	2	3	4	5	6
1						
2						
3						
4						
5						
6						

ABC puzzle number 24A

How many clues will you require to solve the puzzle?

The better you are at solving this puzzle, the fewer clues you will need.

Row   Across

1   The number of letters between the C's is 3.

2   First B is not adjacent to second C.

3   Second B is adjacent to second C.

4   Second A is not adjacent to second C.

5   Second C comes before second B.

6   First A is not adjacent to second C.

Column   Down

1   First A is not adjacent to second C.

2   First B comes after first C and second B comes after second C.

3   The two C's are not adjacent.

4   First B is not adjacent to first C.

5   First C comes before second A.

6   The last square contains a C.

Falling diagonal   The first B is in square number 3.

Rising diagonal   Second C comes before second B.

	1	2	3	4	5	6
1						
2						
3						
4						
5						
6						

ABC puzzle number 24B

How many clues will you require to solve the puzzle?

The better you are at solving this puzzle, the fewer clues you will need.

Row   Across

1   The second B is in square number 4.

2   The first square contains an A.

3   First B comes before second A.

4   The first A is adjacent to the second A.

5   First B comes before first A and second B comes before second A.

6   The number of letters between the B's is 0.

Column   Down

1   Second C comes before first B.

2   The two A's are adjacent.

3   Second A comes after second B.

4   Neither the first square nor the last square will contain an A.

5   First B comes after first C and second B comes after second C.

6   Second A is adjacent to second B.

Falling diagonal   Second A comes before second C.

Rising diagonal   First C comes before second B.

	1	2	3	4	5	6
1						
2						
3						
4						
5						
6						

ABC puzzle number 24C

How many clues will you require to solve the puzzle?

The better you are at solving this puzzle, the fewer clues you will need.

Row   Across

1   The number of letters between the B's is 0.

2   Second A comes before second C.

3   The two B's are not adjacent.

4   The number of letters between the C's is 1.

5   First B is adjacent to first C.

6   First B comes before first A and second B comes before second A.

Column   Down

1   First B comes after second A.

2   First A is not adjacent to first C.

3   The first C is in square number 2.

4   The two A's are adjacent.

5   Second A is not adjacent to second C.

6   First B comes after first A.

Falling diagonal   The first B is in square number 3.

Rising diagonal   First A comes after second C.

	1	2	3	4	5	6
1						
2						
3						
4						
5						
6						

ABC puzzle number 24D

How many clues will you require to solve the puzzle?

The better you are at solving this puzzle, the fewer clues you will need.

Row	Across
1	Second C comes after first B.
2	The second B is in square number 5.
3	The first B is in square number 3.
4	First A is not adjacent to first B.
5	First position letter - second position letter + third position letter - fourth position letter + fifth position letter - sixth position letter = + (0A)+(2B)+(-2C).
6	First A is adjacent to first C.

Column	Down
1	First A comes after first C and second A comes before second C.
2	Second A is adjacent to first C.
3	Second C comes after first B.
4	First A comes after first B and second A comes after second B.
5	The first square contains a C.
6	Second B is not adjacent to first C.

Falling diagonal	Second C comes after second A.
Rising diagonal	First A is not adjacent to first C.

	1	2	3	4	5	6
1						
2						
3						
4						
5						
6						

ABC puzzle number 24E

How many clues will you require to solve the puzzle?

The better you are at solving this puzzle, the fewer clues you will need.

Row	Across
1	Neither the first square nor the last square will contain a B.
2	First B is not adjacent to second C.
3	First A comes before second C.
4	The first B is in square number 2.
5	The first three consecutive squares will contain three different letters.
6	The first A is in square number 3.

Column	Down
1	First A comes before first B.
2	First A comes before first C and second A comes before second C.
3	The two C's are not adjacent.
4	The first C is in square number 5.
5	First A comes after first C.
6	First B comes after first A.

| Falling diagonal | No two squares containing the same letter are adjacent. |
| Rising diagonal | Neither the first square nor the last square will contain a C. |

	1	2	3	4	5	6
1						
2						
3						
4						
5						
6						

ABC puzzle number 24F

How many clues will you require to solve the puzzle?

The better you are at solving this puzzle, the fewer clues you will need.

Row   Across

1   Second C comes before second A.

2   The number of letters between the C's is 2.

3   First C comes after first A and second C comes after second A.

4   First A comes after second C.

5   The two C's are not adjacent.

6   First C comes after first B and second C comes after second B.

Column   Down

1   Second A is not adjacent to second B.

2   The last square contains a B.

3   Second B is adjacent to first C.

4   First C comes after first B.

5   First B comes before second A.

6   First C comes before second A.

Falling diagonal   First B comes after first A.

Rising diagonal   Second C comes before second B.

	1	2	3	4	5	6
1						
2						
3						
4						
5						
6						

ABC puzzle number 25A

How many clues will you require to solve the puzzle?

The better you are at solving this puzzle, the fewer clues you will need.

Row   Across

1   First C comes before second A.

2   First B comes before first A.

3   First A is not adjacent to first B.

4   The first and last squares will contain an A.

5   First C comes before first B.

6   First B comes before second A.

Column   Down

1   Second A is not adjacent to second B.

2   First A comes before second B.

3   Second A is adjacent to second C.

4   The first C is in square number 2.

5   First C comes before first B and second C comes before second B.

6   The two B's are not adjacent.

Falling diagonal   First A comes after first B and second A comes after second B.

Rising diagonal   First B comes after first A and second B comes after second A.

	1	2	3	4	5	6
1						
2						
3						
4						
5						
6						

ABC puzzle number 25B

How many clues will you require to solve the puzzle?

The better you are at solving this puzzle, the fewer clues you will need.

Row   Across

1   First C comes after first B and second C comes before second B.

2   First C comes after first A and second C comes after second A.

3   First A is not adjacent to second C.

4   First A comes before first B and second A comes after second B.

5   First A comes before first B and second A comes before second B.

6   The second B is in square number 5.

Column   Down

1   First A comes before First C.

2   First A comes after first C.

3   First position letter - second position letter + third position letter - fourth position letter + fifth position letter - sixth position letter = + (0A)+(0B)+(0C).

4   First B comes before second C.

5   The two C's are not adjacent.

6   The second A is in square number 4.

Falling diagonal   First A is not adjacent to first C.

Rising diagonal   First B comes after first A.

	1	2	3	4	5	6
1						
2						
3						
4						
5						
6						

ABC puzzle number 25C

How many clues will you require to solve the puzzle?

The better you are at solving this puzzle, the fewer clues you will need.

Row   Across

1   Second A is adjacent to second C.

2   Second B is adjacent to first C.

3   Second A comes after first B.

4   The number of letters between the C's is 0.

5   The two B's are not adjacent.

6   First C comes before first A.

Column   Down

1   First A is not adjacent to first B.

2   No two squares containing the same letter are adjacent.

3   First B comes before second C.

4   The number of letters between the A's is 4.

5   First B is adjacent to second C.

6   Second A comes after first B.

Falling diagonal   The two C's are not adjacent.

Rising diagonal   The first three consecutive squares will contain two different letters.

	1	2	3	4	5	6
1						
2						
3						
4						
5						
6						

ABC puzzle number 25D

How many clues will you require to solve the puzzle?

The better you are at solving this puzzle, the fewer clues you will need.

Row   Across

1   Second A is not adjacent to first C.

2   First position letter - second position letter + third position letter - fourth position letter + fifth position letter - sixth position letter = + (0A)+(2B)+(-2C).

3   Second A is not adjacent to second B.

4   Two of the four groups of three consecutive squares will contain three of the same letter.

5   The second B is in square number 6.

6   First B comes before first A and second B comes after second A.

Column   Down

1   Second C comes after first A.

2   The first B is in square number 4.

3   Second A is adjacent to second C.

4   The number of letters between the C's is 1.

5   No two squares containing the same letter are adjacent.

6   First C comes before first A and second C comes after second A.

Falling diagonal   Second B is adjacent to first C.

Rising diagonal   First A is adjacent to first C.

	1	2	3	4	5	6
1						
2						
3						
4						
5						
6						

ABC puzzle number 25E

How many clues will you require to solve the puzzle?

The better you are at solving this puzzle, the fewer clues you will need.

Row   Across

1   Second C comes after second A.

2   The first three consecutive squares will contain two different letters.

3   First C comes after first A.

4   The number of letters between the A's is 4.

5   First B comes after second C.

6   First A comes after first B and second A comes before second B.

Column   Down

1   Second A is adjacent to first C.

2   First B comes after second C.

3   The second C is in square number 5.

4   Second B is adjacent to second C.

5   The first square contains a C.

6   The second C is in square number 6.

Falling diagonal   Second A comes after first B.

Rising diagonal   First A comes before first B and second A comes before second B.

	1	2	3	4	5	6
1						
2						
3						
4						
5						
6						

ABC puzzle number 25F

How many clues will you require to solve the puzzle?

The better you are at solving this puzzle, the fewer clues you will need.

Row   Across

1   First A comes after first C.

2   Neither the first square nor the last square will contain an A.

3   The two A's are not adjacent.

4   First C comes after first B and second C comes before second B.

5   First A is not adjacent to first B.

6   The first B is in square number 2.

Column   Down

1   The first B is in square number 1.

2   Second C comes before first B.

3   The first A is in square number 1.

4   The first C is in square number 2.

5   First B comes after second C.

6   First C comes before first A and second C comes after second A.

Falling diagonal   Neither the first square nor the last square will contain an A.

Rising diagonal   First B comes after first A and second B comes after second A.

	1	2	3	4	5	6
1						
2						
3						
4						
5						
6						

ABC puzzle number 26A

How many clues will you require to solve the puzzle?

The better you are at solving this puzzle, the fewer clues you will need.

Row   Across

1   First A comes before first B and second A comes before second B.

2   Second A comes after first C.

3   The number of letters between the B's is 1.

4   First B comes after first C and second B comes before second C.

5   First C comes before second B.

6   Neither the first square nor the last square will contain a C.

Column   Down

1   First A comes before first B.

2   First A is not adjacent to first B.

3   First B comes before second C.

4   The number of letters between the B's is 0.

5   The second B is in square number 4.

6   Second C comes after first A.

Falling diagonal   The two B's are not adjacent.

Rising diagonal   The second B is in square number 4.

	1	2	3	4	5	6
1						
2						
3						
4						
5						
6						

ABC puzzle number 26B

How many clues will you require to solve the puzzle?

The better you are at solving this puzzle, the fewer clues you will need.

Row	Across
1	First B comes before second C.
2	The first C is in square number 2.
3	The two A's are not adjacent.
4	The second C is in square number 6.
5	First A comes after first C and second A comes after second C.
6	The first three consecutive squares will contain three different letters.

Column	Down
1	Second A comes before second C.
2	The first B is in square number 1.
3	The number of letters between the B's is 2.
4	First C comes before second A.
5	Second C comes after first B.
6	First B comes after second A.

Falling diagonal   First A is not adjacent to second B.

Rising diagonal   Second B is not adjacent to second C.

	1	2	3	4	5	6
1						
2						
3						
4						
5						
6						

ABC puzzle number 26C

How many clues will you require to solve the puzzle?

The better you are at solving this puzzle, the fewer clues you will need.

Row   Across

1   First A is not adjacent to second C.

2   The number of letters between the A's is 0.

3   Neither the first square nor the last square will contain a C.

4   First A is not adjacent to second C.

5   Second A comes after first B.

6   Second C comes after first A.

Column   Down

1   First B comes after first A and second B comes after second A.

2   Second A comes after first B.

3   The first three consecutive squares will contain three different letters.

4   The two B's are adjacent.

5   First A comes after first B and second A comes after second B.

6   The number of letters between the C's is 2.

Falling diagonal   First C comes after first A and second C comes before second A.

Rising diagonal   First A comes after first B.

	1	2	3	4	5	6
1						
2						
3						
4						
5						
6						

ABC puzzle number 26D

How many clues will you require to solve the puzzle?

The better you are at solving this puzzle, the fewer clues you will need.

Row   Across

1   Second A is not adjacent to second B.

2   First A is adjacent to second C.

3   The second B is in square number 4.

4   First B comes before second C.

5   Second A comes after first C.

6   The number of letters between the B's is 4.

Column   Down

1   The last square contains a B.

2   First A is adjacent to second C.

3   The first square contains an A.

4   Second A comes after first B.

5   First A is adjacent to first B.

6   The first square contains a C.

Falling diagonal   Second B is not adjacent to second C.

Rising diagonal   First A comes before second C.

	1	2	3	4	5	6
1						
2						
3						
4						
5						
6						

ABC puzzle number 26E

How many clues will you require to solve the puzzle?

The better you are at solving this puzzle, the fewer clues you will need.

Row   Across

1   Second, third, and fourth squares will contain three different letters.

2   First B is adjacent to first C.

3   First A comes before First C.

4   The first C is in square number 1.

5   The number of letters between the C's is 0.

6   Neither the first square nor the last square will contain an A.

Column   Down

1   The two C's are adjacent.

2   First A is not adjacent to first C.

3   Second B is adjacent to second C.

4   First B is adjacent to second C.

5   The first square contains a B.

6   Second A is not adjacent to first C.

Falling diagonal   The first A is in square number 1.

Rising diagonal   The second A is in square number 5.

	1	2	3	4	5	6
1						
2						
3						
4						
5						
6						

ABC puzzle number 26F

How many clues will you require to solve the puzzle?

The better you are at solving this puzzle, the fewer clues you will need.

Row   Across

1   Second A is not adjacent to second C.

2   First B comes before first C.

3   First A comes before first B.

4   First B comes after first C and second B comes before second C.

5   First B comes after first C and second B comes after second C.

6   First B comes before first C.

Column   Down

1   First A comes before second C.

2   The number of letters between the A's is 1.

3   The two C's are not adjacent.

4   The two A's are adjacent.

5   Second A is adjacent to second B.

6   First B comes after first A.

Falling diagonal   First B comes before second A.

Rising diagonal   The last square contains a C.

	1	2	3	4	5	6
1						
2						
3						
4						
5						
6						

ABC puzzle number 27A

How many clues will you require to solve the puzzle?

The better you are at solving this puzzle, the fewer clues you will need.

Row   Across

1   First A is not adjacent to second B.

2   No two squares containing the same letter are adjacent.

3   First B comes after first A.

4   Second B is not adjacent to first C.

5   First position letter - second position letter + third position letter - fourth position letter + fifth position letter - sixth position letter = + (-2A)+(0B)+(2C).

6   First B comes before first C.

Column   Down

1   Second B is not adjacent to first C.

2   The number of letters between the A's is 0.

3   Second A is not adjacent to second B.

4   First A is not adjacent to first C.

5   First A comes before second C.

6   First A is not adjacent to second B.

Falling diagonal   Second A is not adjacent to first C.

Rising diagonal   First B comes before first A.

70

	1	2	3	4	5	6
1						
2						
3						
4						
5						
6						

ABC puzzle number 27B

How many clues will you require to solve the puzzle?

The better you are at solving this puzzle, the fewer clues you will need.

Row   Across

1   First A is not adjacent to first B.

2   Second C comes after second A.

3   First A comes before first C and second A comes before second C.

4   Second C comes after second B.

5   First B comes after first A and second B comes after second A.

6   First A is adjacent to second B.

Column   Down

1   The first C is in square number 4.

2   The second A is in square number 5.

3   First C comes before second B.

4   Second C comes before second B.

5   First B is not adjacent to second C.

6   The first and last squares will contain an A.

Falling diagonal   Second C comes before second A.

Rising diagonal   First B is not adjacent to second C.

	1	2	3	4	5	6
1						
2						
3						
4						
5						
6						

ABC puzzle number 27C

How many clues will you require to solve the puzzle?

The better you are at solving this puzzle, the fewer clues you will need.

Row   Across

1   Second C comes before second A.

2   The two B's are not adjacent.

3   The second B is in square number 5.

4   First A comes before first B.

5   First A comes before first B and second A comes before second B.

6   First A comes after first B.

Column   Down

1   Second C comes after first A.

2   First B comes before first A and second B comes before second A.

3   First C comes before first A.

4   The two B's are not adjacent.

5   First B comes before second C.

6   Second B is adjacent to second C.

Falling diagonal   First A comes after first B.

Rising diagonal   Second A comes after second B.

	1	2	3	4	5	6
1						
2						
3						
4						
5						
6						

ABC puzzle number 27D

How many clues will you require to solve the puzzle?

The better you are at solving this puzzle, the fewer clues you will need.

Row   Across

1   Second B is adjacent to first C.

2   First A comes before second B.

3   Second A is not adjacent to second B.

4   Second C comes after first A.

5   Second C comes after first A.

6   First B is adjacent to first C.

Column   Down

1   Second A is adjacent to first C.

2   Second C comes after second B.

3   Second B is not adjacent to first C.

4   The second B is in square number 4.

5   The last square contains a B.

6   First B is not adjacent to second C.

Falling diagonal   The number of letters between the A's is 2.

Rising diagonal   First A comes before First C.

73

	1	2	3	4	5	6
1						
2						
3						
4						
5						
6						

ABC puzzle number 27E

How many clues will you require to solve the puzzle?

The better you are at solving this puzzle, the fewer clues you will need.

Row   Across

1   The first B is in square number 1.

2   First B comes after first A and second B comes after second A.

3   First B comes before first C.

4   The first A is in square number 2.

5   First B is not adjacent to second C.

6   First A comes after first B.

Column   Down

1   Second B is adjacent to second C.

2   First A comes after second B.

3   The second C is in square number 6.

4   First A comes after first B.

5   First A is not adjacent to second C.

6   First position letter - second position letter + third position letter - fourth position
        letter + fifth position letter - sixth position letter = + (0A)+(0B)+(0C).

Falling diagonal   First C comes before first A.

Rising diagonal   First C comes after first A and second C comes before second A.

	1	2	3	4	5	6
1						
2						
3						
4						
5						
6						

ABC puzzle number 27F

How many clues will you require to solve the puzzle?

The better you are at solving this puzzle, the fewer clues you will need.

Row   Across

1   Second B is adjacent to first C.

2   First A comes before first C and second A comes before second C.

3   First A comes before first B and second A comes before second B.

4   First C comes before second A.

5   The first three consecutive squares will contain three different letters.

6   First B comes before first A and second B comes before second A.

Column   Down

1   First B comes before first C.

2   The second C is in square number 6.

3   Second A comes before second B.

4   The second A is in square number 6.

5   Second A comes after first C.

6   Second A is not adjacent to first C.

Falling diagonal   First A is not adjacent to first B.

Rising diagonal   First C comes after first A.

	1	2	3	4	5	6
1						
2						
3						
4						
5						
6						

ABC puzzle number 28A

How many clues will you require to solve the puzzle?

The better you are at solving this puzzle, the fewer clues you will need.

Row   Across

1   The first C is in square number 5.

2   The first A is in square number 1.

3   First A comes after first B and second A comes before second B.

4   First A comes before second C.

5   The number of letters between the B's is 1.

6   First A comes after first C and second A comes after second C.

Column   Down

1   The first three consecutive squares will contain three different letters.

2   The number of letters between the C's is 3.

3   Second A comes before second C.

4   First B is not adjacent to first C.

5   First A comes before second B.

6   First B comes before first A.

Falling diagonal   First A comes after first C.

Rising diagonal   First C comes after first B.

	1	2	3	4	5	6
1						
2						
3						
4						
5						
6						

ABC puzzle number 28B

How many clues will you require to solve the puzzle?

The better you are at solving this puzzle, the fewer clues you will need.

Row   Across

1   The last square contains a C.

2   The first A is in square number 1.

3   Second A comes before second B.

4   First B is adjacent to first C.

5   First position letter - second position letter + third position letter - fourth position

        letter + fifth position letter - sixth position letter = + (-2A)+(2B)+(0C).

6   First C comes after first B.

Column   Down

1   No two squares containing the same letter are adjacent.

2   Second A is adjacent to second B.

3   The first three consecutive squares will contain two different letters.

4   First A comes before second B.

5   First B is adjacent to first C.

6   The number of letters between the B's is 0.

Falling diagonal   Second A comes after second C.

Rising diagonal   First C comes before second B.

	1	2	3	4	5	6
1						
2						
3						
4						
5						
6						

ABC puzzle number 28C

How many clues will you require to solve the puzzle?

The better you are at solving this puzzle, the fewer clues you will need.

Row   Across

1   The number of letters between the A's is 0.

2   Second A comes before second B.

3   First A comes after first B and second A comes before second B.

4   First A comes before first C and second A comes after second C.

5   Second C comes before second A.

6   First C comes after first B.

Column   Down

1   First C comes before second A.

2   The second A is in square number 5.

3   Second C comes after first A.

4   First A comes before second B.

5   First C comes before second B.

6   First position letter - second position letter + third position letter - fourth position letter + fifth position letter - sixth position letter = + (0A)+(0B)+(0C).

Falling diagonal   First C comes before first A and second C comes before second A.

Rising diagonal   The first three consecutive squares will contain three different letters.

	1	2	3	4	5	6
1						
2						
3						
4						
5						
6						

ABC puzzle number 28D

How many clues will you require to solve the puzzle?

The better you are at solving this puzzle, the fewer clues you will need.

Row   Across

1   First B comes before first C and second B comes before second C.

2   The first A is in square number 1.

3   Second A comes after first B.

4   Second A comes after first C.

5   The number of letters between the B's is 1.

6   Second A comes after second C.

Column   Down

1   The second B is in square number 6.

2   The number of letters between the B's is 0.

3   The two C's are not adjacent.

4   First B comes before first A.

5   Second C comes before second B.

6   The first A is in square number 5.

Falling diagonal   Second C comes before second A.

Rising diagonal   The number of letters between the A's is 1.

79

	1	2	3	4	5	6
1						
2						
3						
4						
5						
6						

ABC puzzle number 28E

How many clues will you require to solve the puzzle?

The better you are at solving this puzzle, the fewer clues you will need.

Row   Across

1   First B comes before second C.

2   First B is adjacent to first C.

3   The number of letters between the B's is 3.

4   First A is adjacent to first B.

5   The second C is in square number 4.

6   Second A comes after first C.

Column   Down

1   First C comes after first A.

2   The number of letters between the B's is 0.

3   The second A is in square number 3.

4   First A is not adjacent to second B.

5   First A comes before second B.

6   First B comes before second A.

Falling diagonal   The first C is in square number 2.

Rising diagonal   First B is not adjacent to second C.

	1	2	3	4	5	6
1						
2						
3						
4						
5						
6						

ABC puzzle number 28F

How many clues will you require to solve the puzzle?

The better you are at solving this puzzle, the fewer clues you will need.

Row   Across

1   Second B is not adjacent to second C.

2   First B is adjacent to first C.

3   First A comes before second B.

4   First A comes before first C and second A comes after second C.

5   First A comes after first C and second A comes after second C.

6   First B comes before first A and second B comes before second A.

Column   Down

1   Second C comes after first B.

2   First A comes before second B.

3   Second A is adjacent to first C.

4   Second A comes before second B.

5   First C comes before first B.

6   Second A is not adjacent to second B.

Falling diagonal   Second A is adjacent to second B.

Rising diagonal   First A comes before first C and second A comes before second C.

81

	1	2	3	4	5	6
1						
2						
3						
4						
5						
6						

ABC puzzle number 29A

How many clues will you require to solve the puzzle?

The better you are at solving this puzzle, the fewer clues you will need.

Row   Across

1   Second A is not adjacent to second B.

2   First C comes after first B.

3   Second B is not adjacent to first C.

4   The first square contains a C.

5   Second B is adjacent to second C.

6   The number of letters between the B's is 4.

Column   Down

1   First A comes before second C.

2   The second C is in square number 6.

3   Second A comes before first C.

4   First A is not adjacent to second B.

5   First A is not adjacent to first B.

6   First A is not adjacent to second C.

Falling diagonal   First C comes before first A.

Rising diagonal   First B comes before first C.

	1	2	3	4	5	6
1						
2						
3						
4						
5						
6						

ABC puzzle number 29B

How many clues will you require to solve the puzzle?

The better you are at solving this puzzle, the fewer clues you will need.

Row   Across

1   The two C's are not adjacent.

2   First B comes before first C and second B comes before second C.

3   First A comes before First C.

4   First C comes before first A and second C comes before second A.

5   The number of letters between the C's is 0.

6   Second B is not adjacent to first C.

Column   Down

1   First A comes before second C.

2   Second A comes after first C.

3   First C comes after first A and second C comes after second A.

4   The first C is in square number 4.

5   The first A is in square number 1.

6   Second A is not adjacent to second C.

Falling diagonal   The two C's are not adjacent.

Rising diagonal   First B comes before second C.

	1	2	3	4	5	6
1						
2						
3						
4						
5						
6						

ABC puzzle number 29C

How many clues will you require to solve the puzzle?

The better you are at solving this puzzle, the fewer clues you will need.

Row	Across
1	First C comes before first B.
2	First B comes after first A and second B comes after second A.
3	The two C's are not adjacent.
4	The last square contains an A.
5	Second A comes after second B.
6	Second A comes after first B.

Column	Down
1	The second C is in square number 4.
2	First A comes before second C.
3	First B comes before first A and second B comes before second A.
4	Second C comes after second B.
5	First B comes after First C.
6	Second A comes after first B.

Falling diagonal	Second A is not adjacent to first C.
Rising diagonal	First A comes after first B.

	1	2	3	4	5	6
1						
2						
3						
4						
5						
6						

ABC puzzle number 29D

How many clues will you require to solve the puzzle?

The better you are at solving this puzzle, the fewer clues you will need.

Row   Across

1   Second B is not adjacent to first C.

2   Second B is adjacent to first C.

3   First C comes after first A and second C comes after second A.

4   First A is adjacent to second C.

5   Second A comes after second B.

6   Second C comes after first B.

Column   Down

1   The first square contains a C.

2   The first B is in square number 1.

3   First position letter - second position letter + third position letter - fourth position letter + fifth position letter - sixth position letter = + (0A)+(0B)+(0C).

4   First B comes before first C.

5   Second A comes after first C.

6   First A comes after first C.

Falling diagonal   First A is not adjacent to second B.

Rising diagonal   The number of letters between the A's is 0.

	1	2	3	4	5	6
1						
2						
3						
4						
5						
6						

ABC puzzle number 29E

How many clues will you require to solve the puzzle?

The better you are at solving this puzzle, the fewer clues you will need.

Row   Across

1   The first and last squares will contain a C.

2   First A is not adjacent to second C.

3   First A comes before first B and second A comes before second B.

4   Second A is not adjacent to second C.

5   First A comes before first C and second A comes after second C.

6   Second A is not adjacent to first B.

Column   Down

1   First B comes after second A.

2   Second A comes after first C.

3   First B comes before first C and second B comes before second C.

4   First C comes after first A and second C comes before second A.

5   First A comes before second C.

6   Second C comes before first A.

Falling diagonal   Second A comes before second B.

Rising diagonal   Second A comes before second B.

	1	2	3	4	5	6
1						
2						
3						
4						
5						
6						

ABC puzzle number 29F

How many clues will you require to solve the puzzle?

The better you are at solving this puzzle, the fewer clues you will need.

Row   Across

1   The two A's are adjacent.

2   The second B is in square number 4.

3   Second A is adjacent to first C.

4   First A comes after first C and second A comes after second C.

5   First A is adjacent to first C.

6   Second A comes before second B.

Column   Down

1   The two A's are adjacent.

2   The first three consecutive squares will contain three different letters.

3   Second A is not adjacent to second C.

4   First B is not adjacent to first C.

5   First A is not adjacent to first B.

6   Second C comes before second B.

Falling diagonal   First B comes after first A and second B comes after second A.

Rising diagonal   Only one of the four groups of three consecutive squares will

                                contain three different letters.

87

	1	2	3	4	5	6
1						
2						
3						
4						
5						
6						

ABC puzzle number 30A

How many clues will you require to solve the puzzle?

The better you are at solving this puzzle, the fewer clues you will need.

Row   Across

1   Neither the first square nor the last square will contain a B.

2   First A comes after first C.

3   First A comes before first B.

4   Second A is not adjacent to first B.

5   The first A is in square number 2.

6   Neither the first square nor the last square will contain a B.

Column   Down

1   First B comes before second A.

2   The second B is in square number 6.

3   Second C comes after second A.

4   First B comes before second C.

5   The first A is adjacent to the second A and the first B is adjacent to the second B.

6   The second C is in square number 6.

Falling diagonal   First B comes after First C.

Rising diagonal   Second A comes before first C.

	1	2	3	4	5	6
1						
2						
3						
4						
5						
6						

ABC puzzle number 30B

How many clues will you require to solve the puzzle?

The better you are at solving this puzzle, the fewer clues you will need.

Row   Across

1   First A is adjacent to first B.

2   The number of letters between the C's is 0.

3   Second A is not adjacent to first B.

4   Second A comes after first C.

5   First B comes before first A.

6   The number of letters between the B's is 0.

Column   Down

1   First A comes before second B.

2   The number of letters between the B's is 4.

3   The first B is in square number 3.

4   First B comes after first C and second B comes before second C.

5   Second C comes after first B.

6   First C comes before first A and second C comes after second A.

Falling diagonal   First B is not adjacent to second C.

Rising diagonal   The second A is in square number 2.

	1	2	3	4	5	6
1						
2						
3						
4						
5						
6						

ABC puzzle number 30C

How many clues will you require to solve the puzzle?

The better you are at solving this puzzle, the fewer clues you will need.

Row   Across

1   First A comes before First C.

2   The first A is in square number 3.

3   First A comes after first C.

4   First B is adjacent to first C.

5   The two A's are not adjacent.

6   Second C comes after second B.

Column   Down

1   The first A is in square number 1.

2   First B comes before first A and second B comes after second A.

3   Second A is not adjacent to second C.

4   Second A is not adjacent to first B.

5   First A comes before second C.

6   First C comes before first B.

Falling diagonal   The number of letters between the C's is 3.

Rising diagonal   First A comes before first C and second A comes before second C.

	1	2	3	4	5	6
1						
2						
3						
4						
5						
6						

ABC puzzle number 30D

How many clues will you require to solve the puzzle?

The better you are at solving this puzzle, the fewer clues you will need.

Row   Across

1   Second C comes after first A.

2   The number of letters between the B's is 0.

3   The last square contains an A.

4   First A is not adjacent to first B.

5   First B comes before first A and second B comes after second A.

6   First B comes before second A.

Column   Down

1   First A comes before first B.

2   First C comes before second A.

3   Second A is not adjacent to first C.

4   Second B is adjacent to second C.

5   Second B is not adjacent to second C.

6   First A is adjacent to first B.

Falling diagonal   First B comes after first C and second B comes before second C.

Rising diagonal   Second C comes after second B.

	1	2	3	4	5	6
1						
2						
3						
4						
5						
6						

ABC puzzle number 30E

How many clues will you require to solve the puzzle?

The better you are at solving this puzzle, the fewer clues you will need.

Row   Across

1   First A is not adjacent to first C.

2   First B comes after first A.

3   First A is adjacent to first B.

4   Some group of three consecutive squares will contain three different letters.

5   The number of letters between the C's is 0.

6   The number of letters between the A's is 2.

Column   Down

1   The second C is in square number 3.

2   Second B is not adjacent to first C.

3   First A comes before first B and second A comes before second B.

4   First C comes before first B and second C comes after second B.

5   First position letter - second position letter + third position letter - fourth position letter + fifth position letter - sixth position letter = + (0A)+(0B)+(0C).

6   The number of letters between the A's is 0.

Falling diagonal   First C comes after first A and second C comes after second A.

Rising diagonal   Second A comes before second C.

	1	2	3	4	5	6
1						
2						
3						
4						
5						
6						

ABC puzzle number 30F

How many clues will you require to solve the puzzle?

The better you are at solving this puzzle, the fewer clues you will need.

Row   Across

1   First A comes before First C.

2   First B is not adjacent to first C.

3   The first B is adjacent to the second B.

4   First B comes before first A and second B comes before second A.

5   First B comes before first A and second B comes after second A.

6   Second A is adjacent to first C.

Column   Down

1   First C comes before second B.

2   First C comes before second A.

3   First position letter - second position letter + third position letter - fourth position letter + fifth position letter - sixth position letter = + (0A)+(0B)+(0C).

4   The second B is in square number 4.

5   First A comes after first B and second A comes after second B.

6   First B is not adjacent to second C.

Falling diagonal   First C comes after first A.

Rising diagonal   First C comes before first B.

Solution 16

	1	2	3	4	5	6
1	B	A	A	C	B	C
2	A	A	B	C	C	B
3	B	C	C	B	A	A
4	C	B	A	A	C	B
5	C	B	C	A	B	A
6	A	C	B	B	A	C

Solution 17

	1	2	3	4	5	6
1	B	A	A	C	B	C
2	A	C	C	B	B	A
3	C	B	A	A	C	B
4	A	C	B	B	C	A
5	B	A	C	C	A	B
6	C	B	B	A	A	C

Solution 18

	1	2	3	4	5	6
1	A	A	B	B	C	C
2	A	C	C	B	A	B
3	C	B	A	A	B	C
4	C	B	B	C	A	A
5	B	C	A	C	B	A
6	B	A	C	A	C	B

Solution 19

	1	2	3	4	5	6
1	A	C	B	B	A	C
2	C	B	A	C	B	A
3	B	A	C	A	C	B
4	B	C	C	A	A	B
5	C	B	A	C	B	A
6	A	A	B	B	C	C

Solution 20

	1	2	3	4	5	6
1	A	B	B	C	C	A
2	C	B	A	B	A	C
3	A	A	C	C	B	B
4	C	A	B	B	C	A
5	B	C	C	A	A	B
6	B	C	A	A	B	C

Solution 21

	1	2	3	4	5	6
1	B	B	A	C	C	A
2	B	A	B	A	C	C
3	A	B	C	B	A	C
4	C	A	B	C	A	B
5	C	C	A	A	B	B
6	A	C	C	B	B	A

Solution 22

	1	2	3	4	5	6
1	B	A	B	C	C	A
2	C	B	A	A	B	C
3	A	B	C	B	A	C
4	A	C	C	A	B	B
5	B	A	A	C	C	B
6	C	C	B	B	A	A

Solution 23

	1	2	3	4	5	6
1	C	B	A	A	C	B
2	B	A	C	B	A	C
3	A	C	B	C	B	A
4	A	C	B	B	C	A
5	B	A	C	C	A	B
6	C	B	A	A	B	C

Solution 24

	1	2	3	4	5	6
1	C	A	B	B	C	A
2	A	A	C	B	B	C
3	A	C	B	A	C	B
4	C	B	C	A	A	B
5	B	C	A	C	B	A
6	B	B	A	C	A	C

Solution 25

	1	2	3	4	5	6
1	B	C	A	A	C	B
2	B	A	B	C	A	C
3	A	C	B	B	C	A
4	A	B	C	C	B	A
5	C	A	C	B	A	B
6	C	B	A	A	B	C

Solution 26

	1	2	3	4	5	6
1	A	B	A	C	B	C
2	B	C	B	C	A	A
3	A	B	C	B	C	A
4	C	A	A	B	B	C
5	C	C	B	A	A	B
6	B	A	C	A	C	B

Solution 27

	1	2	3	4	5	6
1	B	B	C	C	A	A
2	A	C	A	B	C	B
3	A	B	A	C	B	C
4	C	A	B	B	A	C
5	C	A	B	A	C	B
6	B	C	C	A	B	A

Solution 28

	1	2	3	4	5	6
1	B	A	A	B	C	C
2	A	C	B	A	B	C
3	C	B	A	A	C	B
4	A	B	C	C	A	B
5	C	A	B	C	B	A
6	B	C	C	B	A	A

Solution 29

	1	2	3	4	5	6
1	C	B	B	A	A	C
2	A	A	B	B	C	C
3	A	C	A	B	C	B
4	C	B	A	C	B	A
5	B	A	C	C	B	A
6	B	C	C	A	A	B

Solution 30

	1	2	3	4	5	6
1	A	B	A	C	B	C
2	C	C	A	A	B	B
3	C	A	B	B	C	A
4	B	C	C	B	A	A
5	B	A	C	C	A	B
6	A	B	B	A	C	C

Kermit Rose lives in Tallahassee Florida.
He majored in mathematics at Florida State
University and worked at the Florida State
University Computing Center.

Mathematics has remained a strong hobby for
Kermit all his life. He is eminently qualified
to design novel puzzles.

He got the idea of the ABC puzzle book
because his cousin showed him an example of
one, and then he realized that he could make
a book of similar puzzles, but easier to solve
than the one his cousin showed him.